YOU ARE HERE

ALSO BY JENNY LAWSON

Furiously Happy

Let's Pretend This Never Happened

YOU ARE HERE

An Owner's Manual for Dangerous Minds

JENNY LAWSON

(Crayons & matches not included, but recommended)

FLATIRON
BOOKS
NEW YORK

YOU ARE HERE. Text and illustrations copyright © 2017 by Jenny Lawson. All rights reserved. Printed in the United States of America. For information, address Flatiron Books, 175 Fifth Avenue, New York, N.Y. 10010.

www.flatironbooks.com

The Library of Congress Cataloging-in-Publication Data is available upon request.

ISBN 978-1-250-11988-9 (trade paperback)

Our books may be purchased in bulk for promotional, educational, or business use. Please contact your local bookseller or the Macmillan Corporate and Premium Sales Department at 1-800-221-7945, extension 5442, or by e-mail at MacmillanSpecialMarkets@macmillan.com.

First Edition: March 2017

10 9 8 7 6 5 4 3 2 1

This book is dedicated to my chronic anxiety.

You are *literally* always there for me, and you accidentally forced me to make this book to help save me from you. You deserve a vacation.

No, really. Go. We're fine here.

And more importantly, it's dedicated to the people on the Internet who sit with me (in spirit) while I hide away from the world. You have the key to my pillow fort. Always.

Care and Feeding of This Book

Hello.

This is your book. You may pick it up and immediately realize that it's yours, or you may glance through it and wonder what sort of mentally unstable person vandalized all this perfectly good paper. And the answer is me. *I'm* the mentally unstable person in this book, and that's a good thing because you will either be able to totally relate to it or it will make you feel better about yourself in comparison.

"I could have written this book!" you might yell to yourself indignantly. And yes, you could have. And you will. Because there is space purposely left here for you to complete it. So technically *you* are the co-creator of this book. Which means you're to blame too. Sorry. That's just how books like this work.

I'm mainly known as a writer, but when I was on the book tour for *Furiously Happy* (a humorous memoir about my own battles with mental illness) I often found myself trapped in hotel rooms waiting out anxiety attacks. And to keep my own hands from hurting me I started doodling. It's something I've done since I was a kid as a form of meditation . . . drawing and filling in the empty spaces with patterns and faces and words that I needed to get out of my head or pound into my head. I shared a few online and was shocked at the response . . . people asking if they could have copies . . . to color, to frame, to tattoo onto their bodies to remind them that they aren't alone. And somehow the small magic I used to keep myself whole and safe stretched out and enveloped others.

People came through signing lines with books, but more and more often they came with prints of my drawings, which had touched them or given them insight into the mind of a loved one who didn't always fit in the world. And that's how this book was born. It's a combination of notes from the road, advice I've learned and have been given, pictures for when words aren't there, and words to explain pictures that baffle some and speak to others. It's filled with empty spaces and places for you to write in your own notes and thoughts and sketches. It's ready to be colored or traced or hung up. It's ready to be destroyed or improved. It is true art therapy, which is a lot like real therapy, but less expensive and messier. Plus, this is therapy you can do while hiding in your pillow fort in your bed, whereas real therapists would consider having to meet in your bed a setback. Unless you have a weird therapist who is encouraging you to meet them in bed, in which case I suspect there's an issue and you should look at their credentials and possibly call the police.

I had a hard time coming up with the name for this book. The original title was *"The Secret Guidebook.* Not that the guidebook is secret. It's for sale in a store. That's the opposite of secret. But I want it to be a guide to your secrets. To help you explore them, I mean. Not an actual guide to locating your physical secrets. There are no maps showing where you buried the bodies. I would never do that to you. This book is the antithesis of that. It's a place to discover your secrets, or store your secrets, or burn your secrets. Or forget your secrets and just use it as a coaster. It's your book, dude. Whatever works best for you. I'VE GOT YOUR BACK."* But then I thought, *Jesus, this is way too long for a subtitle. I can't even fit my name on the cover. Let's start over.* So I did and I came up with *YOU ARE HERE.*

And it works for a number of reasons.

---

* There were actually a number of titles in the running for this book, but my favorite was DON'T POISON EVERYONE. I liked it because it's good advice and also because each person reading it puts their own emphasis on the words and that's a really good psychological test. For example, my editor thought it was just common knowledge that you shouldn't kill people, but technically I was putting the emphasis on the word "everyone," because if you poison *everyone* you are totally going to get caught. Plus, that's a dick move and makes for a shitty inspirational book. Make good choices. Don't poison *everyone*. In fact, you shouldn't poison anyone. I mean, unless they really deserve it. Like, if it's a serial killer who ate your cocker spaniel and kicked your granny you could maybe send him a tuna casserole where the mayo had been sitting out too long. That seems fair. Also, you could emphasize the word "poison" in the title and then it becomes "Don't *poison* everyone." Which is also good advice because most people don't deserve to be poisoned. Some people just need to be junk punched. Some need to be stabbed with a fork. Some just need a stern look and a sigh that says "I'm disappointed because I expected better from you." There are different levels of actions for different types of assholes. And these are exactly the important things that most self-help books leave out. But not this one. You chose correctly, my friend. Good job.

Firstly, because you *are* here. Right now as you are reading this, you are here. I've got you. It's like I'm magic. Also, you're thinking of a number between 3 and 5. That number is 4. MAGIC! And *yes*, it's hard for you to be thinking of a number that's not 4 when I'm making you read that the number is 4 but it's still a pretty crafty trick and you should be glad we didn't have money riding on it because you'd owe me a dollar right now.

Secondly, *YOU ARE HERE* works because it's something I've been teaching myself over the years that has helped me deal with a mind that's a bit broken. Sometimes it's because of depression or anxiety or stress or just life being an asshole, but one of the most valuable things I've learned is the importance of recognizing the moment. Of saying to yourself, "I am here right now. Here is a moment to take a breath and realize that I am still alive, that I'm surviving, and that even if things are dark, they will get better. It's a moment to remind myself of the things I appreciate and take for granted. It's a moment to look up and realize that one day I'll want to come back to this spot and the only way to do that is to live in that moment entirely so it doesn't pass me by. I feel the pain and the joy and sometimes the utter lack of emotion in that moment. And I reassess. And I learn."

Each page in this book goes back to a moment. A moment when I grabbed on to a memory that triggered others. A moment when I felt alone. A moment when I realized that being alone is the least alone you can be because everyone feels that way. A moment when I wrote something silly or funny or profound on my arm or napkin or phone and then immortalized it in this book. Some of it is dark. Some is light. Some is silly and profane and irreverent. All of it is life. All of it is happening. Right now. All around you. And you are here for it. And if this book works correctly, it will give you those moments each time you open it.

It is a misfit's atlas, a signpost, a place to escape. It is a guide for safe passage. It's a reminder that here there be dragons. It's an outlet for misdirected energy and creativity and meditation. It's a way to explore yourself, or lose yourself, or find yourself . . . a do-it-yourself starter kit. It's a journey that starts with you.

You are here.

YOU ARE HERE

This is a safe place.

Stay a while.

You are welcome.

Pain is real, whether from depression or anxiety or arthritis or one of the many invisible illnesses that don't really show themselves, but still exist and have to be treated, and—more importantly—have to be believed in order to be treated. If you struggle with mental illness you need to know that your fight is real and your survival is something to be proud of.

Remember that you are needed. Remember that not all things are visible and provable. Love, faith, pain, anxiety, depression, compassion . . . these aren't always quantifiable. They aren't always measurable. They are often invisible. But they are real.

And so are you.

Stay real. Stay alive. Stay vigilant against assholes that make you question yourself. We already get enough of that from the doubting voices in our heads and the lies depression tells us. Listen to my voice, now. You are real. You are worthwhile. You are so important, both in ways you will discover, and in ways you'll never see. You send out needed ripples of greatness and kindness in unexpected and accidental ways.

You won't always see the wonderful ways in which you shift the world. They may be invisible to you. But I promise you they are real.

JUST BECAUSE YOU CAN'T SEE IT DOESN'T MEAN IT'S NOT REAL.

Build your dreams around you. Then build a pillow fort around your dreams. Fill it with cats and books and wine slushies. Then build a fiery moat around your pillow fort, filled with acid and razor blades, because people are going to want that pillow fort. And your dreams, maybe. Mostly the pillow fort, though. Maybe you should build your pillow fort in another location so you're more diversified and you have a place to fall back on if looters get in. I don't know. I'm not an expert on real estate. This isn't even about real estate. It's about dreams.

Stay focused, y'all.

Sometimes people
come into your life
just to teach you
how not to become them.

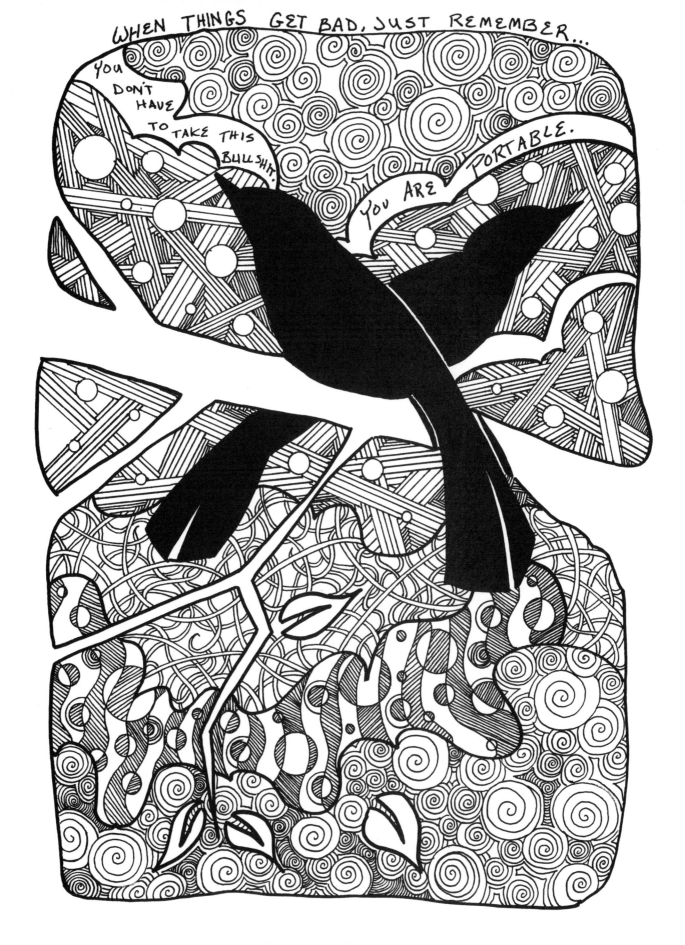

Weird on,
you bad-ass motherfucker.

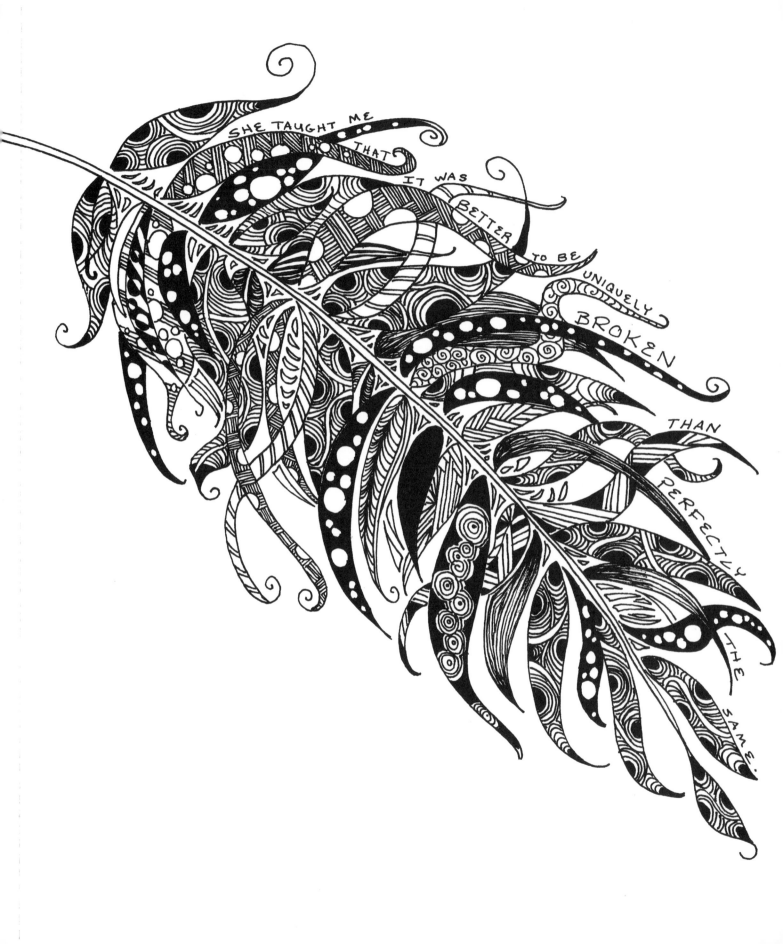

You are not alone.

When my great-grandmother died, we found hundreds of Mason jars filled with her canning in the cellar. Some had gotten too hot and had to be thrown away. It was like throwing away memories or hope or fear or whatever it is that drives us to keep things we don't need, but that a future us might.

The jars of honey were safe, though. Honey lasts forever. Glass jars of golden sunlight, just as sweet as the day they were sealed. Some jars had crystallized in strange shapes. Some held honeycomb and a few stray bees, frozen in time.

Each jar was marked with a day. *March 1, 1934. July 18, 1966.* I ate a day in 1942 that gave me sustenance and energy and the warm glow of life.

We threw away the peaches, poisoned with exposure to time.

Instead we lived in honey . . . golden, and thick with memory.

Sometimes I just need to
be saved from myself.

I AM STITCHED TOGETHER BY CAREFUL HANDS—REMADE FROM THE TORN AND SHREDDED PIECES OF WHO I HAVE BEEN AND WHO I HAVE GROWN OUT OF. I AM BROKEN, BUT I AM MENDED. AND I AM STRONGER BECAUSE OF IT.

I am made up of stitched-together parts and worn-out pieces and small, bright things and memories that bring happiness and sadness, and tiny patches that I picked up along the way and forgot where they came from.

I am made from rips and tears and gentle stitching from myself and loved ones and strangers.

I am a patchwork quilt. Comforting and surprisingly warm. Beautiful from a distance. A pattern of myself. The unconscious code of me.

Most of my favorite people
are cats.

When I was little my anxiety disorder made me afraid of everything. I avoided people and retreated into books. I would do anything to stay out of the spotlight.

My teachers often told me to "stop being a frightened little rabbit." I'm sure they meant well, but when you have anxiety disorder you avoid a lot of life. You find joy in books or art or things you can do in hiding. Sometimes that gives people the wrong idea. They think that you're a frightened little rabbit. They think that the fear you battle makes you weak, but in fact, it makes you strong.

You fight through fear every moment. Every day. The worry never completely ceases, but you keep reaching out to find your life, and to live it and love it. That takes courage. A learned courage that has to be sustained and practiced. And sometimes you hide away because the fear wins for a bit . . . but soon you'll turn your hand to life again, even knowing the consequences. I *am* a frightened little rabbit, it's true. But anyone who has spent time raising rabbits knows this often-forgotten truth . . . *frightened rabbits fight the hardest*. They know when to trust and when to run. They pick their battles. They survive tough odds even though they are constant prey for anything bigger than they are. They are cute and adorable, but if you fuck with them they will scratch your goddamn eyes out.

When I was in 3rd grade I had a rabbit named "Pootie McGee" who was a total snuggle-monster, but when the cat got too close to us Pootie freaked the shit out and scratched the hell out of my face, using his tiny but almost magically powerful back legs to get to higher ground (i.e., the top of my head). I had a scar on my face for a month that looked like I'd been in a knife fight. And I had, in a way. I looked like a tiny bad-ass you shouldn't fuck with because of another tiny and easily underestimated bad-ass.

I *am* a frightened rabbit. And if you don't think that's something to respect then you are *seriously* underestimating me.

"SMALL" IS NOT THE SAME AS "WEAK." ALWAYS REMEMBER, FRIGHTENED RABBITS FIGHT HARDEST.

What is it about night that makes things grow?

At night the fever rises. The sickness worsens. The party rages louder. The laughter grows. The fighting escalates. The monsters come out. Every small sound becomes an echoing roar. The ocean rises and the wind picks up. The lightning brightens. The loneliness is palpable. The dreams are longer and stronger and so are we. And weaker. And more fragile. We are more of everything, all at once.

When the end comes I suspect it will come at night, when the veil between us and infinity is at its thinnest. We look up and see the stars, the same ones we'd see a million miles away. We become lonely astronauts in our unique, small vessels. We rise up like unsteady balloons. There are less illusions to keep us tethered to earth and so we rise. Our voices. Our senses. We stretch out, unaware that we are doing so. Unaware that this fear of falling comes from night. From falling off the world.

In the daytime we can convince ourselves that we are big. We are important in our unimportance. We are ignored by God and seen by few. We are hidden and small and made unafraid because of it. But at night we see the farthest reaches of space. We see infinity. We do not reflect back. There is no us in our sight. There are only stars. There is only forever. And as we stretch out we feel the terrible pull of infinity in those dark hours. We lengthen and grow, and in doing so we can look back at our feet and realize how incredibly small we really are.

We belong to darkness. We belong to infinity. We raise our voices in the vacuum of control and we try to fill the emptiness, but it will not work.

We are the emptiness. We are infinity.

We rise.

THE NIGHT IS SHARP AND JAGGED.
IT WILL NOT LAST.

NEVER DOUBT
THE MORNING COMES.

Let's grow weird together.

I love Shel Silverstein, but I've never understood the appeal of *The Giving Tree*. It's supposed to be a tale of self-sacrifice but it always struck me as a super abusive relationship. The tree gives this kid her apples and the boy eventually chops her limbs off and hollows her trunk out and then dumps her in the ocean. *That's real serial killer shit, y'all.*

Sometimes I work too hard or give too much and I become that tree. And it makes sense. If you give too much of yourself you can't recover. You're worthless except as a stump for some habitual user to rest his ass on. Sometimes self-care and restraint and giving yourself the ability to say "no" is the only way to keep yourself strong enough (and *you* enough) in order to keep giving, and to feel happy in giving rather than feeling exhausted and taken advantage of. Plus, if you say "no" every once in a while you won't have to wonder if you inadvertently created a serial killer because you were too nice of a tree to say, "NO, ACTUALLY I DON'T WANT YOU TO DECAPITATE ME." (That last sentence seems like a strange, random string of words, but I'm keeping it because maybe you need to hear it. Friends don't let friends become decapitated trees.)

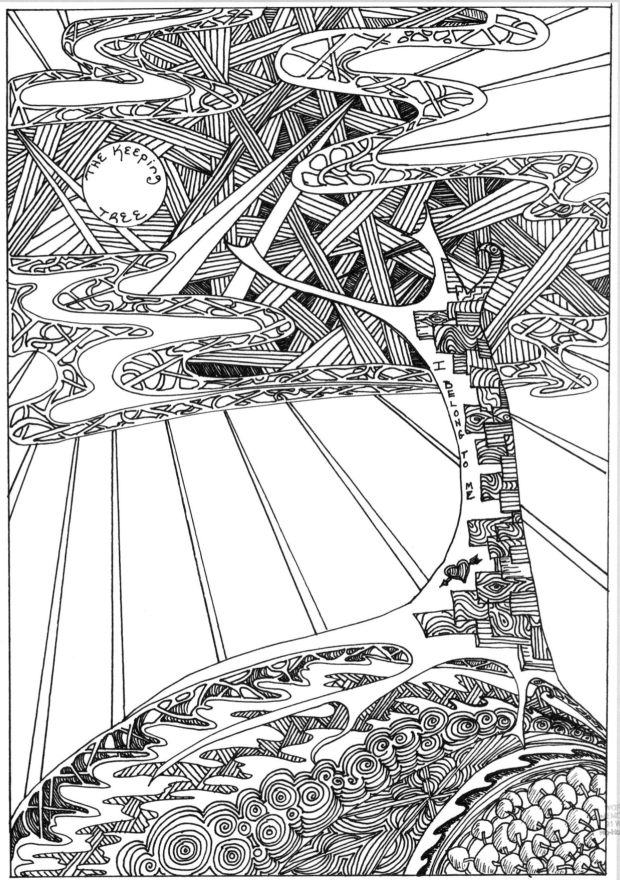

THE KEEPing TREE

I BELONG TO ME

This picture didn't start out black.

It started with a drawing I couldn't quite finish. In frustration I wrote, "I'M NOT FINISHED YET" across the bottom. But it struck me as having a greater meaning because I'm *not* finished yet, even when my mind tells me to quit. It felt so therapeutic that I wrote it again and again, like a demented Bart Simpson, until the page was black. Until I realized just how much more I still want to do. Which left me with this black page. A place where I could write my darkest confessions and fears and they would sink—invisible—into the dark paper. A portable confession booth. A safe space for honesty.

Write down your fears with a black pen, or just trace them with your finger. Or scream them loud with Wite-Out—the very stuff meant to cover up mistakes but now used to shout. Keep them and use them to make you stronger. Or kill them forever by tearing them out of this book and watching them burn.

Those words are yours. They belong to you. Everyone has secrets. A past. A bad choice. Regrets. Guilt. Doubts we don't admit out loud. The things we hide that make us who we are. Sometimes they turn us cold. Sometimes they make us brittle. But almost always they come with the capacity to give us compassion and kindness. It is a very strange kindness, but a special one. And the biggest kindness is in forgiving yourself, and comforting yourself, and realizing that you are human and perfectly flawed and so much more than just the sum of your parts. It's in showing yourself the same compassion you'd give to those you love if they confessed the very things you hide from the world. You deserve that kindness.

Do whatever feels right. There is no wrong answer. It's a time to unpack. Unburden. No judgment.

You are here.

But you are not alone.

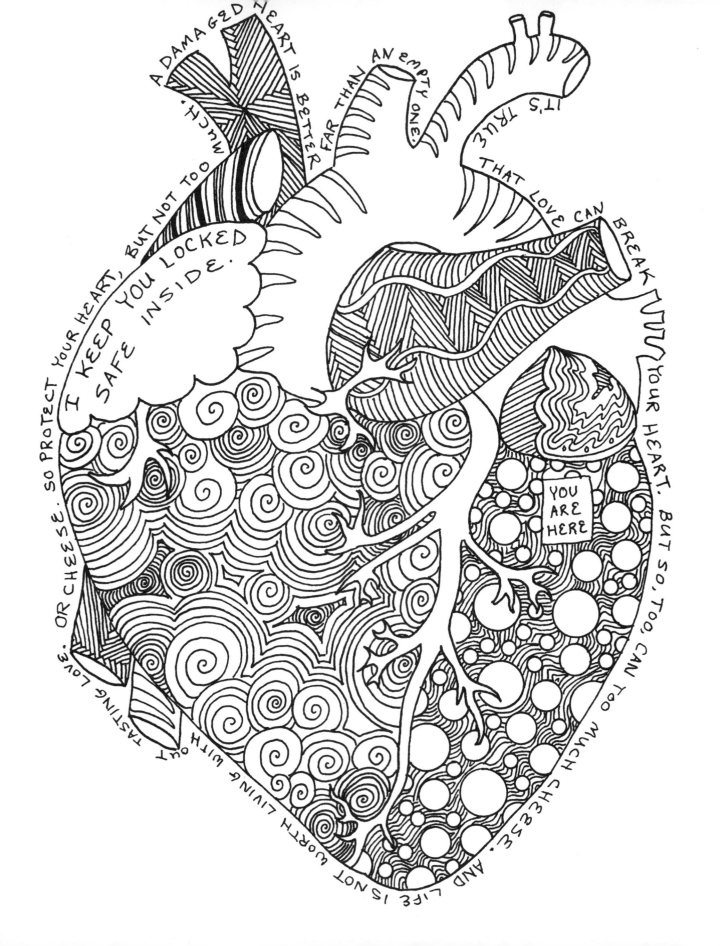

Yesterday, I bought a shirt and the rack said "slightly irregular" and the price tag said "slightly off," and I thought that it would have been more accurate if those things were written on the front of my shirt, but still, I'll take it.

Also, it was on sale for some reason.

YOU WILL GET THROUGH THIS.

Reading this entitles you to one wish.

But? It is a wish for a stranger.

One you will never meet.

One who will never know you wished it for them.

Go now. Close your eyes.

Make a wish for a stranger.

Good.

Whatever it was that you wished for?

You deserve that too.

And I wish it for you.

And that's how the world turns.

Show me what makes you
a misfit and I will show you
what makes you necessary.

Write Down Five Outrageous Things You've Done

Not all of them have to be true, and at least one should be a lie so that if the police ever get their hands on this they can't use it against you.

The lovely thing is that when your future relatives find this list they will be intrigued and possibly even a little scared, but that just adds to your mystery and will probably keep them from fucking with you when you're elderly and you just want some damn peace and quiet.

I'll give you my five first so you can feel better by comparison.*

----

* This list cannot be used against me in court because I do not give the police permission to read it. Are you a cop? You know you have to tell me if you are, right? Wait, you don't? Really? When did that start? ALWAYS? Jesus. I gotta go add that to Snopes. Thanks for the info, copper. You're one of the good ones.

I'll Go First So You Know It's Safe

1. I spent most of 1995 in the Yucatán, attempting to save the endangered damp sewer-cooter, a warrior-like furry water mammal with a terrible name. I was not successful and that's why people say they don't exist today.

2. I was named an official czar of Texas after an award show refused to let me bring a donkey to a red carpet event despite the fact that I totally should have been able to. This injustice was made more palatable when the mayor gave me a crown, scepter, and proclamation listing my title as the "czar of nothingness." The proclamation was signed with the paw print of the stray cat that lives at city hall, whom I report to directly.

3. One time I made a human without even using an instruction manual. Like, hair, fingernails, all that jazz. It was a tiny human, but still, it was like making a clone except I did it inside my body where I couldn't even see anything. Science!

4. My cousin and I were arrested for illegally transporting our Uncle Jesse's moonshine and part of our probation stated that we couldn't own guns so instead we carried around compound bows tipped with dynamite. We had this bad-ass '69 Dodge Charger that we drove over cliffs to escape from the corrupt police in the county. Later we painted over the Confederate flag on the roof because in hindsight it seemed kinda racist.

5. I wanted to visit a primate sanctuary in my neighborhood that houses famous primates who have retired from fame, but they wouldn't let me hang out with the monkeys because "We're not a zoo" but then I bought them a disco ball because chimpanzees love disco and then they were like "Wow. You really *do* know primates. Yeah. Come on over."

Okay. Now it's your turn.
Write down five outrageous things you've done.
(At least one of which is a lie.)

The great thing about making this list is that it frees you up creatively to come up with some things you really wouldn't mind accomplishing. Look at your list. Are the things you didn't actually do things that you really *want* to do? Then go do them. If you doubt yourself then just look at the real things on your list you've already accomplished. Now you have goals.

Or maybe you look at your list and thank God that you avoided all the scandals and terrible choices that you invented to throw everyone else off. Either way? You win.

Conclusion? This might be the best self-help book ever.

YOUR TURN

1._____

_____

_____

_____

2._____

_____

_____

_____

3._____

_____

_____

_____

4._____

_____

_____

_____

5._____

_____

_____

_____

Happiness doesn't always last.

But neither does sadness.

I drew this when I felt certain I'd never feel joy again. A month later I looked at it again and wondered how I had ever felt that way.

Depression lies.

Don't believe it.

I DON'T ALWAYS REMEMBER WHAT HAPPY LOOKS LIKE. BUT I THINK IT FELT LIKE THE SUN... ...AND TASTED LIKE HONEYSUCKLE...

We are gentle souls.
But if you fuck with us we will cut you.
And we will eat your face meat.

Not all of it. Just enough to let you know we mean business. *Is it illegal?* No idea.
I can't keep up with all the laws in each state. I go with my gut and keep a good
lawyer on retainer. What I do know is that face chewing is the mark that shows
where our people have been. It's also the mark that shows that you were once a
real asshole to one of us. But we don't hold it against you. Every day is fresh and
we forgive as easily as we eat face meat. Which is to say, grudgingly and hesitant-
ly, constantly questioning if it's the right thing to do. *

---

*Y'all? *Don't actually eat other people's faces.* It's most likely illegal and face meat is probably disgusting and
all cartilagy. This whole thing is just an urban legend to make assholes less likely to fuck with us. Don't let
them see this note or the jig is up. I tell you this because face gnawing is a slippery slope to cannibalism.
And also because you might wrongly judge a wonderful someone with a giant bite mark on his face who was
actually not attacked by us, a peaceful people who at most will whack you with a piñata stick or lightly stab
someone with a fork. Go talk to the person with the face bite mark. He might be fascinating and maybe a
shark bit him while he was saving orphaned kittens he was teaching to swim. Who knows? Either way you're
probably in for a good story. Unless he says he was bitten in the face meat by one of us. Then he's a dirty liar
and you should brandish your fork at him until he realizes the terrible mistake he's made.

START HERE

SO MAYBE ONLY 1% OF US ARE SOCIALLY-AWKWARD MISFITS, BUT THAT 1% SHOULD BE USED SPARINGLY, LIKE WASABI, OR DYNAMITE. JESUS AM I STILL RAMBLING? SORRY. I DON'T GET OUT MUCH, AND NEITHER COULD WE. GET US TOGETHER AND WE ARE A FORCE TO BE RECKONED WITH. HANDLE US FOR MORE THAN AN HOUR AT A TIME. AND PEOPLE AND WE ALL NEED TO GO HOME AND RECOVER AND READ OR BINGE-WATCH TV UNTIL OUR MEDS KICK IN. BUT THAT'S OKAY BECAUSE YOU COULDN'T MAGNIFICENT AND STRANGE AND POWERFUL ENOUGH TO CHANGE THE WORLD. BUT PROBABLY ONLY FOR AN HOUR AT A TIME BECAUSE IT IS EXHAUSTING TO BE AROUND

SHE ALWAYS FELT FAR TOO AFRAID FOR ADVENTURES, BUT THAT WAS OK BECAUSE MISADVENTURE WAS HER TRUE CALLING.

I'm not always good at everything.

But I am very good at being me.

There are worlds inside of you.

Wonderful and terrible and
brilliant worlds.

WE ARE ALL MADE UP OF STARDUST. AND MEAT. AND BACTERIA. AND SONGS THAT GET STUCK IN YOUR HEAD WHEN YOU'RE TRYING TO SLEEP. AND SKITTLES IF YOU JUST ATE SKITTLES. AND PROBABLY OTHER THINGS. I DON'T KNOW. I'M NOT GOOD AT SCIENCE.

Everyone is mad.

Everyone is hurt.

Your hurt doesn't make you
unique or special.

But what you do with it does.

Think of the most intimidating person alive.

Today that person pooped. And then they probably looked at their own poop afterward.

And if they didn't poop today they probably wished they had and they hope that tomorrow they will.

Not so intimidating now, are they?

Also, they likely farted four times today.

Just saying.

He THOUGHT HE WAS NOTHING.

NORMAL. IGNORABLE. INSIGNIFICANT. UNIMPORTANT.

HE DID NOT KNOW THAT THE FANTASTIC DREAMS HE HAD WERE MORE BRILLIANT THAN ANY ART THAT WILL EVER BE SEEN. HE DID NOT KNOW THAT THE SONGS THAT CAME TO HIM IN THE SHOWER WOULD PASS FROM ONE PERSON TO THE NEXT UNTIL THEY WERE MADE INTO SONATAS THAT INSPIRED THE WORLD.

HE DID NOT KNOW THAT ONLY HE COULD SEE A COLOR THAT NOONE ELSE COULD SEE.

HE DID NOT KNOW THAT HE WAS SPECIAL...

... AND YET HE WAS.

People always say, "Remember, no matter how bad it gets, someone else has it worse," and that's certainly true, but it doesn't make your shit any better. In fact, it only reminds you that no matter how shitty things are, they could get worse. Instead we should say, "Remember, no matter how good things get, someone else has it better." That way we feel less guilty for our blessings and also we get a reminder that things can get brighter. Or if they don't, that there's someone we can rob who we won't feel too bad stealing from because he has it better than us.

Although once we steal his stuff he'll be the one hearing that "someone else has it worse off." But we'll be there to stop that nonsense and remind him that *plenty* of people have things better and maybe we should go steal *their* golden Ferraris from them. And eventually we'd all end up in jail, but I bet we'd get out of prison because you can't fit that many people in jail and also no jury is ever on the side of a douchebag that owns a solid-gold Ferrari.

So we'll be fine . . . as long as there are people out there who have it better than us.

IF DANDELIONS ONLY BLOOMED IN RARE PLACES THEY'D BE MORE VALUABLE THAN ORCHIDS.

I always thought I'd like to be a dandelion—those vivid yellow flowers that bloom in the cracks of sidewalks or abandoned lots. Anything that thrives in such strange, broken places holds a special kind of magic. It shines bright and golden for a moment before it withers, but then—when most have given it up for dead—it explodes into an elaborate globe of spiderweb seedlings so fragile that a wind or a wish sends it to pieces.

But the falling apart isn't the end.

It depends on the falling apart.

Its fragility lets it be carried to new places, to paint more gold in the cracks.

I always thought I'd like to be a dandelion.

But I think, in a way, I already am.

I. WILL. BURY. YOU.

(In kindness.)

Perhaps the most selfless
thing you can do today is to
be kind to yourself.

"SOMETIMES I FEEL...HOLLOW," I WHISPERED.

"OF COURSE YOU FEEL EMPTY," SHE SMILED. "IF YOU WERE FULL YOU'D BE DONE."

"EMPTY" IS HOW YOU KNOW YOU STILL HAVE ROOM FOR LIFE.

This is a secret guide.

Not that the guide itself
is secret.

It's a guide to my secrets.
And maybe yours.

Look for the elbow. That's how you high-five. Seriously. Just look at the elbow of the person you're high-fiving. Now you won't miss their hand. It doesn't make sense but it's true. Looking at the hand is the worst place to look because what you're looking for is in motion and won't be there when you think. It's like solving a story problem in your head. The elbow controls the hand, though. So just look at the elbow. And that's the best advice I ever got.

My husband, Victor, complained that this picture was "too harsh," but I explained that what I meant was that if you drag me down I will cut you *loose*. Or cut you *free*. But also, if it was bad enough I'd probably physically cut you, so I guess technically we're both right.

When I was drawing this fingerprint it felt off because I like to draw things straight and true, or with graceful curves that I erase and redraw until they are closer to perfect, but fingerprints aren't like that. They aren't perfect or beautiful. They are irregular and asymmetrical and jagged and swirled and patterned in a non-patterned way. But I kept coming back to this drawing to finish it because there was something beautiful in the ugliness. It's not until you pull back and see the big picture that you can see how the imperfections make up the pattern. That you can see the forest. The path. The elegance that comes from the way that all of these broken and bent and ungraceful pieces come together to make something beautiful and perfect.

And I guess that's what life is about. It's ugly and weird when you look close up, but then you see the big picture later on and you realize the pattern wouldn't have been complete without the horror and the jagged little edges. Life is made from these bits and we'd be incomplete without them.

They make us who we are.

They make us unique.

They make us beautiful.

They make us match up with others but never completely. They make us *us*.

Sometimes all you can do is surrender to the pattern you're given and make beauty in every space you can.

Because the pieces that come together in swirls and breaks and broken pieces are your signature. They are your fingerprints.

They are you.

And if you look at them with the right set of eyes, they are beautiful.

IF THINGS GET UGLY JUST SPLATTER RED PAINT ALL OVER THIS SO IT LOOKS LIKE A CRIME SCENE. THAT WAY IT WILL INTIMIDATE NORMAL PEOPLE AND NO ONE WILL FUCK WITH YOU. IT'S NEVER NOT AWESOME. UNLESS YOU GET ARRESTED. CARRY BAIL MONEY JUST IN CASE. THAT'S JUST GOOD ADVICE.

YOU ARE HERE

Listen to the tiny voice
inside your head.

Unless it's trying to tell you
that you're worthless.

Then, fuck that voice.
That voice is an asshole.

IT IS POSSIBLE TO BE

STANDING ON THE TOP OF THE WORLD AND ALSO BARELY HANGING ON TO THE EDGE AT THE SAME TIME

JUST HOLD ON —— DON'T LET GO

Surviving the darkest moments
will make you stronger in will,
character, empathy,
compassion, or all four.

You can always see the sun.

Even at night when you look up into the sky you see planets and the moon, but what you really see is the sun reflecting off them. On nights when the sky is dark with clouds, the sun is still there, visible a few miles away or from houses tall enough to pierce the clouds. You can see suns that no longer exist. They sent out light that has been traveling for years just to hit you now. We see suns that lived before we began. Light from suns a million miles away is traveling toward us now, even if you never see it. It'll reach your great-great-granddaughter, perhaps, in a future where you may be a memory, like the light of extinct suns that reaches us now. We're in different time lines in some ways, which is unsettling and comforting all at once.

The sun always shines.

Even if we don't see it.

Even if we don't exist.

Even if it doesn't exist.

A sun still shines.

I'M NOT FEELING QUITE MYSELF TODAY. BUT NOBODY ELSE IS FEELING QUITE LIKE ME EITHER, SO I'M TRYING NOT TO BEAT MYSELF UP ABOUT IT.

I told Victor that the pen is mightier than the sword and he argued that a gun is mightier than both of them. But then I pointed out that I could stab him in the eyes with my pens and then he wouldn't be able to see me to shoot me. And he said that he'd just use sonar and he started making *ping*-ing submarine sounds. I don't think he has real sonar, but he said that he could tell I was still in the passenger seat of the car because of his *ping*-ing. I think it had more to do with the fact that I hadn't stabbed him in the eyes yet. He did have a point though because whales now seem like the scariest animals ever because they can still find you even if they're blind. Then Victor said that a whale with a handgun would be even scarier and I agreed. But Victor said that he could still win in a battle with the armed whale and I just let him have that because he was still *ping*-ing and I was ready to stop talking.

So I drew this whale with a handgun. And by that I mean I drew a whale holding a handgun with my pens. I can't draw with a handgun. No one can. Although I did have a BB gun when I was a kid and I'd shoot smiley faces into paper plates nailed to a tree. Or at least that was what I was trying to do. Mostly it was smiley faces with measles. But then I thought that even more dangerous than a whale with a gun would be a narwhal with a bayonet because it has the same echolocation and weapon but also, it's a fish WITH A KNIFE ON ITS HEAD. *No one's beating that.*

PS. Spell-check changed "I drew a whale with a handgun using my pens" to "I drew a whale with a handgun using my penis." *WTF, spell-check? What is wrong with you?*

Also, when you turn this picture upside down it looks like the whale has passed out from taking too many hits on his crack pipe. So it's a good public service announcement, either way.

PPS. I suggest drawing something on him. Maybe name him or give him a tattoo or some pants. I gave him a sash that says "WORLD DOMINATION OR BUST." But this decision, *as in life*, is completely up to you.

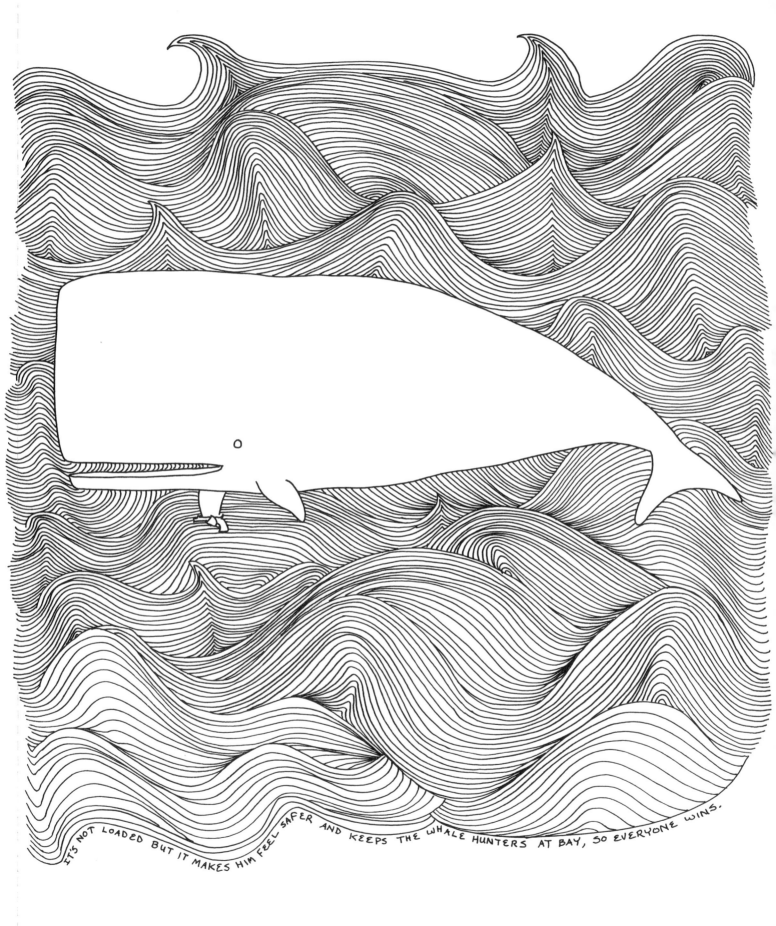

IT'S NOT LOADED BUT IT MAKES HIM FEEL SAFER AND KEEPS THE WHALE HUNTERS AT BAY, SO EVERYONE WINS.

ONE OF THE MOST IMPORTANT HUMAN NEEDS IS TO BE SEEN, ACKNOWLEDGED, AND REMEMBERED.

I SEE YOU.
I SEE YOU AND YOU ARE BEAUTIFUL.

Sometimes we say the
things we mean.

Sometimes we mean the
things we say.

And on rare occasions,
we do both.

Get fucking inspired.

Everything will be all right.

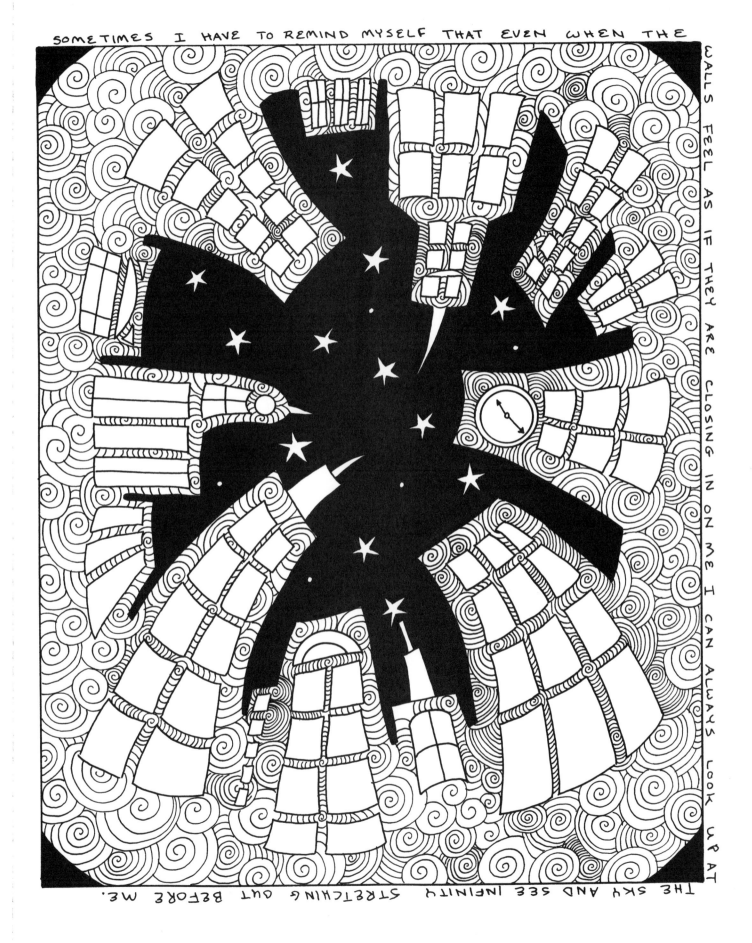

Sometimes I wish I had a dog
named "Tiny Gentleman."

(Sorry. They're not all going
to be winners.)

Every now and then I fall apart a little and I have to hold my arms tightly around myself so I don't spill any of me on you.

SOME PEOPLE WISH FOR EXTRA HANDS BUT I ALREADY DON'T KNOW WHAT TO DO WITH THESE TWO NERVOUS HANDS THAT FLUTTER LIKE FRIGHTENED BIRDS.

Complicated paths beckon me
toward brilliant mistakes and
glorious confusion.

Might as well get lost on an
adventure while I still can.

Not all pain is visible. But not all love is visible either, and that doesn't make it any less real. We believe the pain because we feel it, but we often forget how much we're loved because it doesn't always present itself in ways that make you physically gasp.

It's real, though. And you're soaking in it.

Sometimes I wonder if my
purpose in life is to look for my
purpose in life.

And if so, does that mean that
I'll never succeed
or that I just did?

There is a place in my head filled with the stacks of books I've read and the songs I've heard and the memories that make me who I am. It is a refuge and sanctuary where I keep safe the people I've loved. It is forever a cluttered mess.

But it's *my* mess, and I'm okay with that.

Good pushes more good. Bad creates more bad.

Make good.

Do good.

Be good.

Do not be subservient. Do not be polite. Be *good*. There *is* a difference, and surprisingly often "good" and "polite" are at opposite ends of the spectrum.

This is the place where good and bad meet. This is where they ebb and push and smash together in ways that cause confusion and tragedy and small miracles.

This is where we live. This is all happening now, inside of us and outside of us.

We live in the revolution.

The revolution lives in us.

We are the ever-changing battle, and the winners and the losers.

Once upon a time, there was a girl who forgot the rest of her story so she had to make it up as she went along.

She kept it a secret all of her life. And one day when she was 99 she whispered this very confession to her husband.

He paused and smiled kindly and told her that *everyone* was just making it up as they went along. And she was happy and sad all at once, and also a little bit relieved that she hadn't known it all along.

And that was the end.

I thought that if I surrounded myself with other weirdos I'd seem almost normal, but I've learned that even with other outsiders I don't entirely blend in.

But then I thought, "Why would I ever want to?"

We were meant to be together.

Our strangeness hangs
together so well.

YOU ARE HERE

People say you should listen to your inner voice, but my inner voice is always going on about burning down the garages of people who are mean to me. Maybe I should listen to my inner voice's inner voice. I imagine it just wants love and kindness. And matches, probably. I can never find matches.

Some people say there's no such thing as an inner voice, but who told them that? *Their inner voice*. Those people are liars. Or maybe cyborgs.

Either way, be careful.

And don't let me have any matches.

I don't believe in radical anything. I suspect I'm too lazy to be radical.

I could possibly get behind radical ambivalence.

Maybe.

MY SONG IS NOT ALWAYS BEAUTIFUL, BUT IT IS ALWAYS DISTINCTIVE.

ITS STRANGENESS IS WHAT MAKES IT SPECIAL.

Sometimes silence
is a song.

"Just relax and you'll float," she told me. And I thought she was crazy and trying to kill me, but I guess in a way she was right because dead people float too. So she was being encouraging *and* hedging her bets, and you've kinda gotta respect that.

I REMEMBER NIGHT SWIMMING. THE STARS FELL INTO THE WATER AND I FLOATED, FREELY, CRADLED IN THE SPARKLING DARKNESS LIKE AN UNTETHERED ASTRONAUT.

This is your book.

This is your life.

You are in charge.

This is not the end.

Start again, continue, reinvent
yourself, become the person
I see in you.

Take a deep breath.

We can start whenever you want.

Begin.

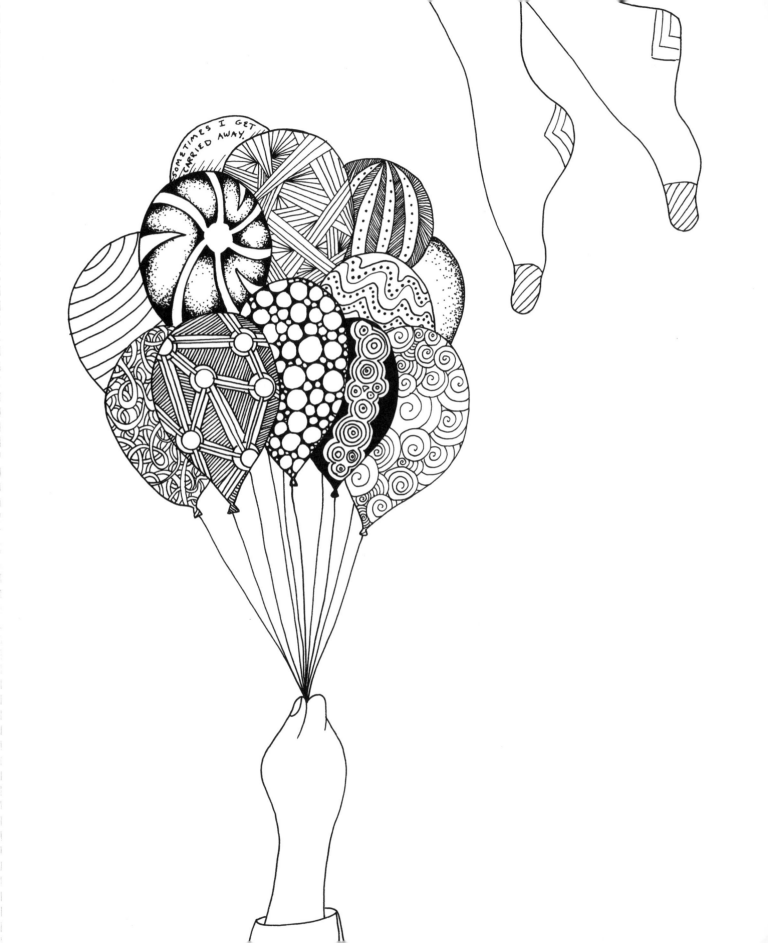

I've always been jealous of Santa. He's hermit-y but still beloved and once a year he goes to visit everyone while they aren't even conscious and then he's like "I'm EXHAUSTED. I have to sleep for a year." He has elves, but I suspect they are his version of cats . . . curling up beside him on the couch and sitting inside all the empty boxes. His yearlong voyeurism of naughty and nice is like me watching reality TV shows and judging everyone there. Plus, he makes an appearance in millions of houses, but only does it if you promise to not look at him. And you have to leave cookies for him at every stop, which is like a delicious paycheck *that he doesn't even have to pay taxes on.* In fact, this is how I'm charging for speaking gigs from now on.

Basically, what I'm saying is that if Santa was here he'd be diagnosed with Avoidant Personality Disorder, just like me, but people still love him. The man is a saint. *Literally.* So I guess the trick is to be crazy long enough that it seems normal and traditional and then no one questions it.

I think I'm on the right path.

If you randomly shout **"QUIT IT"** a few times a day then people who are fucking with you behind your back will think you are psychic and will leave you alone, and people who *aren't* fucking with you will be extra nice to you, because they'll think you're having a breakdown.

Feeling stabby.

Sometimes the best thing
to be sheltered from
is from being sheltered.

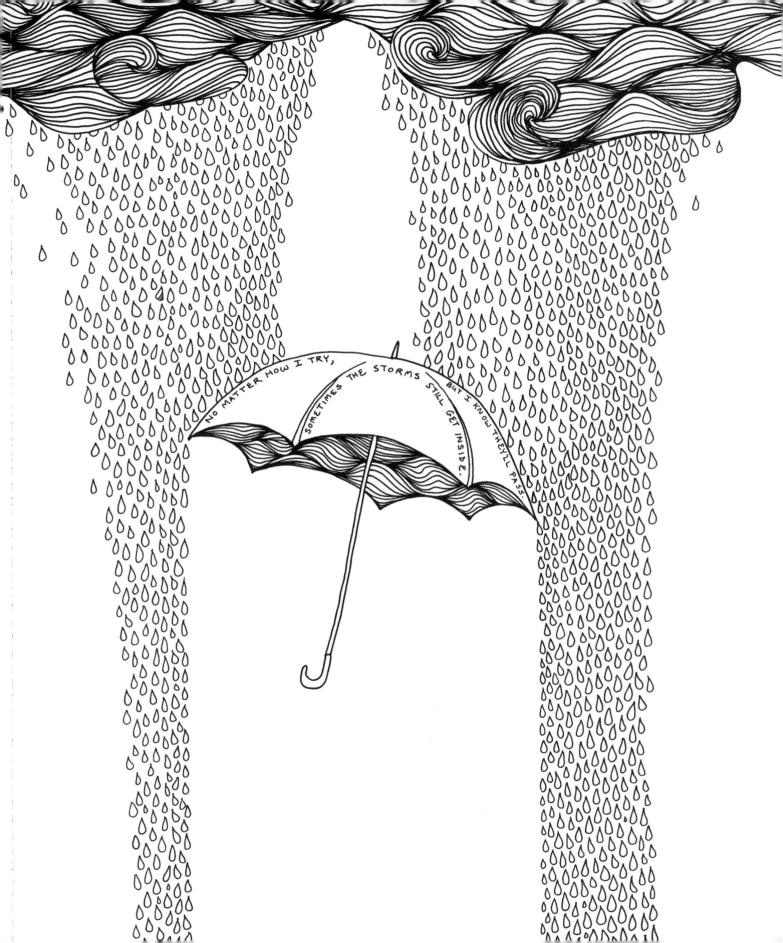

If you're not certain whether you're dealing with a demon, sprinkle a circle of salt around it as a protective barrier. It's possible that it isn't a demon and it's just an asshole, but either way they'll probably leave. People hate it when you keep aggressively salting them.

Be free.

Do stupid things.

Make ridiculous mistakes.

Mortifying yourself gives others the
encouragement to do the same.

Remember, poor choices often make the best stories.

Climb the stairs to the moon.

I don't know how to be right, so I'm running away to join the circus. Except instead of the circus I'm running away to be myself. To grow again and remember how to be the fantastically strange creature I was meant to be.

I'm not finished yet.

Neither are you.

I AM DONE
OWNING THIS PROBLEM.

Some images are made of stories and vice versa.

There is a circle here.

There is a curve that reminds you of your mother's cheek.

There is a line that seems to stretch on forever.

These are the crosshatches that count the days that you've forgotten.

These are the crosshatches that count the days burned into your memory.

These are the marks of the seconds you survived.

This is the leaf you picked up when you were six, which you thought was the most beautiful thing you'd ever seen, but your teacher said to leave it because it was dirty and that you could find another one later.

This is the leaf you found when you were 20. It doesn't shine as brightly, but you don't know if that's because of you or because of the leaf.

This is the shape of the screen door of the house you lived in when you were 12.

This is the back of the neck of the boy you loved.

This is the shape of the voices you wish you could hear again.

This is you.

You are here.

IT'S A MAGIC LAMP,
IT'S A SORCERER'S HAT,
IT'S A TIME MACHINE
AND A SONG BIRD
AND A TREASURE CHEST,
IT'S A WEAPON AND A WEIGHT,
AND ALSO YOU CAN TYPE WITH IT.

TODAY I CHANGED EVERYTHING.

TODAY I TOOK A SHOWER.

TODAY I KEPT BREATHING.

Circle any of the above that apply.
They are all a celebration, y'all.

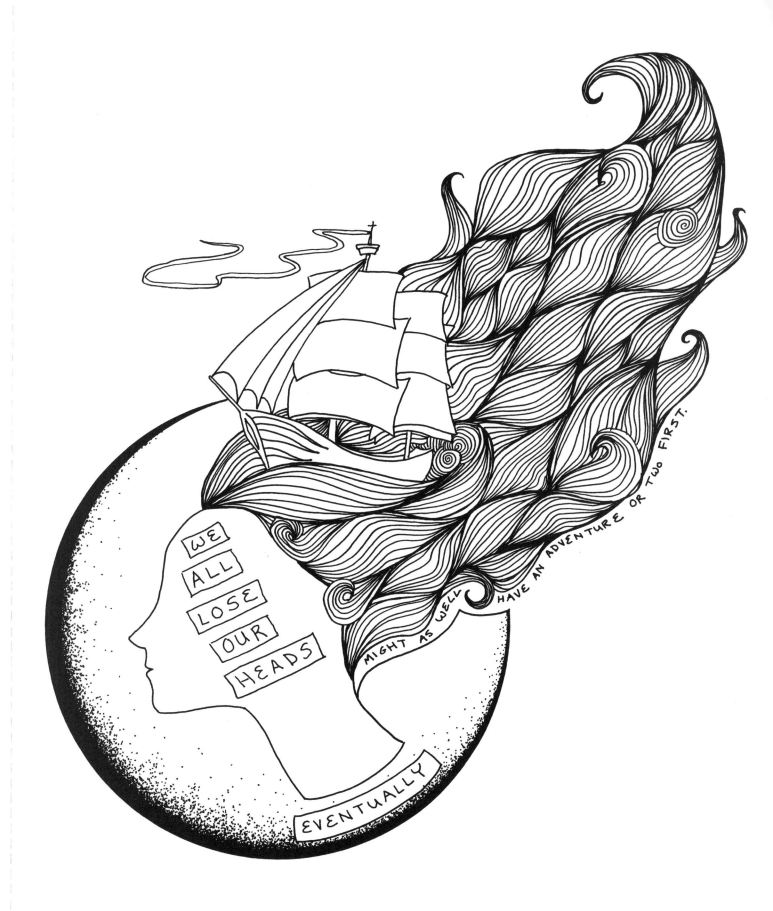

We walked out of the theater and I admitted that I didn't entirely understand it all, but that most of it was utterly brilliant. He agreed that it was confusing but that— all things considered—it was wonderful. Then I confessed that I'd slept through a lot of it, and he said he had too but that he didn't mind so much because the sleeping was some of his favorite parts. Then I asked if we were still talking about the movie and he said he never thought we were.

A prayer for those lost in the dark.

You are not alone.

You are not forgotten.

We keep you in our hearts.

All candles blaze on to light your way safely home.

All lights burn bright in the hope you will feel the shine.

All stars gleam, glittering, to remind you of your own unique shimmer.

The glow beams toward you, radiating. It flickers and flutters, yes. But never doubt, *it comes*.

Back of This Book

You know how there are blank pages in the back of some books? Why is that? Victor says that it's because book people like to fuck you over and make you think you're getting more than what you pay for. I say that it's bonus paper that you can use to write lists of people who have wronged you so you don't forget later exactly why you hate them. It's sort of the glass half-full test of literature and I think it means that Victor is a pessimist and that I have a lot of books that I can't *resell* because they're full of my secrets.

Turns out though that all books have to come in weirdly specific numbers of pages and so even though that last page was technically the end it wasn't a good number so we either have to cut pages to get to the specific number or add pages, so I chose to add so that you could fill the blank pages with stuff like lists of animals you'd be happy to sleep with if it wasn't illegal. Victor just read this and said I need to clarify that I'm referring to adorable wild animals that you would catch shit about if you bought a lot of them to snuggle with. Like the time I tried to rent a dozen otters to play with for the day and the zoo was like, "We don't rent animals. Stop calling" and I was like, "What about the river otters? Are those less endangered than the ocean ones? Because I'm not picky" and they said that wasn't the point so I asked about beavers because those are basically cheap otters and they were like, "We don't even have beavers" and then I was all, "WHY DO ZOOS EVEN EXIST ANYMORE?" and now they're out of business. Or they blocked my number. One of those. The point is that I'm trying to fill all my holes with animals and the world is making it difficult. Emotional holes, I mean. Not my physical holes. Gross. I wouldn't fill my holes with otters. That's illegal and probably causes infections. Wait. I've forgotten what I was talking about.

Oh! I remember. Blank pages. So this is where the blank pages should be, but then I asked if I could fill them with stuff and that's how you ended up with a coloring book that has a bonus after-the-credits Easter egg about why filling your holes with wild animals will give you a urinary tract infection. Blame the book industry for all of this, y'all.

I feel like I should make up for this so I'm going to add a page where you can make your own sketch. Sort of. I mean, technically any blank page is a page where you can make your own doodles but I've always found that one of the hardest parts of starting out a sketch is creating the outline you'll fill in so I'm going to make one for you and you can just fill that shit in. Lines, circles, patterns on wallpaper, words you love…whatever. And if you fuck it up then just scrawl a big anarchy A on it and be all punk rock while screaming: "I DON'T COLOR INSIDE THE LINES, BITCHES. I'M ABOVE THE LAW!"

Whatever.

It's art.

You do you.

Acknowledgments

This book was a bit of heaven and a bit of hell and it refused to move out of the way until it was finished. I felt a bit like I was going mad when I was creating it and even more mad when I wasn't, so I owe thanks to every single person who helped me to push it out of my head and onto paper.

Thank you to Victor and Hailey for being Victor and Hailey. You are my favorite people ever and I don't know what I did to deserve you. Thank you to Maile for inspiring me and understanding me, and thank you to Annie and Emily for teaching me how to high-five properly. (I told you it was important enough to include in a book.) Thank you to my wonderful agent, Neeti Madan, for seeing this strange book as a gift rather than a cry for help. Thank you to Amy Einhorn for believing in me and helping me find my words. Thank you to Marlena and Caroline and Lisa and Mary and Flatiron and everyone else who did the difficult, behind-the-scenes magic that it took to turn a series of journals and doodles and make them into a real, live boy. You are my favorite deadline. Thank you to Stephen, Laura, Karen, Brene, Gemma, Bunmi, Neil, Amanda, Phil, Scalzi, Bonnie, Wil, Anne, Maureen, Doctor Who, the person who invented cheese, and the guy who didn't honk at me even though we both know I totally pulled out in front of him without using my blinker. Thank you to the person I forgot to thank here. Thank you to the girl who

unwittingly said the perfect thing just when I needed it, and thank you to that guy who didn't know he saved me. Thank you to the people in lines and e-mails and comments who encouraged me to do something different even when it seemed scary. Especially when it seemed scary.

Thank you to you. For being here.

You are here, aren't you?

I'm so glad you made it.

DISCARD